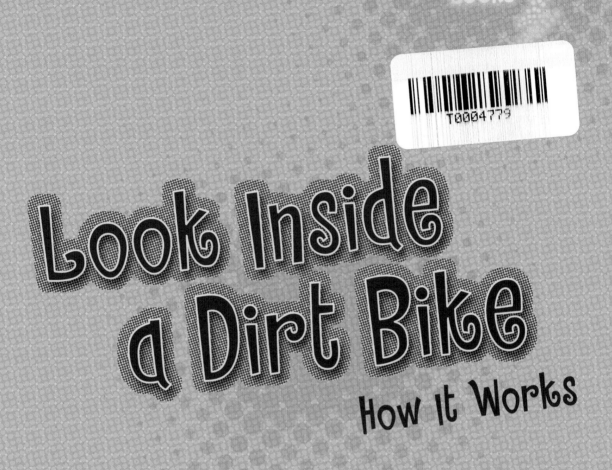

Look Inside a Dirt Bike

How It Works

Brianna Kaiser

Lerner Publications • Minneapolis

Lerner Publications Company
An imprint of Lerner Publishing Group, Inc.
241 First Avenue North
Minneapolis, MN 55401 USA

For reading levels and more information, look up this title at www.lernerbooks.com.

Main body text set in Billy Infant Regular. Typeface provided by SparkType.

Photo Editor: Nicole Berglund

Library of Congress Cataloging-in-Publication Data

Names: Kaiser, Brianna, 1996- author.
Title: Look inside a dirt bike : how it works / Brianna Kaiser.
Description: Minneapolis : Lerner Publications, [2024] | Series: Lightning Bolt Books. Under the hood | Includes bibliographical references and index. | Audience: Ages 6-9 | Audience: Grades 2-3 | Summary: "Dirt bikes can race on almost any terrain! But how do they handle rough trails and obstacles? Readers will learn about the many types of dirt bikes and get an inside look at what happens inside an engine"— Provided by publisher.
Identifiers: LCCN 2023013485 (print) | LCCN 2023013486 (ebook) | ISBN 9798765608357 (library binding) | ISBN 9798765624371 (paperback) | ISBN 9798765615669 (epub)
Subjects: LCSH: Trail bikes—Juvenile literature. | BISAC: JUVENILE NONFICTION / Transportation / Motorcycles
Classification: LCC TL441 .K35 2024 (print) | LCC TL441 (ebook) | DDC 629.227/5—dc23/eng/20230330

LC record available at https://lccn.loc.gov/2023013485
LC ebook record available at https://lccn.loc.gov/2023013486

Manufactured in the United States of America
1-1009521-51489-5/25/2023

Table of Contents

What Are Dirt Bikes?   4

Types and Racing   6

How Dirt Bikes Work   12

Cool Parts   16

Dirt Bike Diagram   20

Tire Treads   21

Glossary   22

Learn More   23

Index   24

What Are Dirt Bikes?

A racer zooms forward. They ride up a jump and soar into the air. What is the racer riding? It's a dirt bike!

Many dirt bikes can ride on muddy tracks.

Dirt bikes are a kind of motorcycle. But they are only used for riding off-road. People ride them for fun or in races.

Types and Racing

Many people around the world compete in dirt bike races. But not all races are the same. That's why there are many kinds of dirt bikes.

A close-up of a dirt bike engine

Dirt bikes have different engine sizes. Dirt bike races separate riders into classes based on their dirt bike's engine size.

Most dirt bikes are lightweight. Being light allows them to move quickly over a track's terrain and obstacles.

A motocross rider in the desert

Dirt bikes can make big jumps during a race.

Motocross dirt bikes can handle off-road tracks with jumps and sharp turns. Supermoto dirt bikes race on tracks with dirt trails and paved roads.

Trail dirt bikes are the most common. They have large gas tanks so they can ride long distances.

Trail dirt bikes can drive on off-road trails for many miles.

Dirt bikes help riders travel on bumpy trails quickly.

Enduro dirt bikes are a mix of motocross and trail. They can speed up quickly and drive on rocky trails. Many have big gas tanks for long races.

How Dirt Bikes Work

A dirt bike's gas is stored in its gas tank. Gas is sent to the engine when the rider turns the throttle.

The engine burns gasoline to create energy to move the wheels. When the rider turns the throttle, the dirt bike moves.

A motocross rider filling his gas tank

A dirt bike's brakes and throttle are on the handles.

A rider uses the handles to steer the dirt bike in the direction they want to go. Turning the handles also turns the front wheel. Brakes stop or slow down the wheels.

Some dirt bikes have knobby treads that are better for riding on rough terrain. Smoother supermoto treads are better for smooth terrain.

Knobby tires help a dirt bike move over muddy or bumpy tracks.

Cool Parts

No matter what track or trail a rider is on, the dirt bike's suspension matters. The suspension is a system that uses springs to help control the bike.

A dirt bike's suspension keeps the dirt bike's tires in contact with the track. It also absorbs shock from the track's bumps, jumps, and obstacles.

The suspension lets riders make big jumps without getting hurt.

New dirt bikes are made every year. They will continue to get better in the future.

Riders from around the world compete in dirt bike races.

Dirt bikes racing in a forest

There are so many dirt bikes to choose from! Which one would you want to ride?

Dirt Bike Diagram

handles

seat

suspension

engine

tires

Tire Treads

It is important for dirt bikes to have good tires. Tires have knobs that increase the dirt bike's grip on the road. When knobs are worn down, they don't grip as well. A rider may not be able to make sharp turns or ride on certain tracks with worn down knobs. Tires are usually good for four to five years.

Glossary

class: a group of riders based on their engine size

energy: the power used to make something work

obstacle: something, such as a jump, that stands in the way of finishing a race

off-road: relating to or done with a vehicle designed especially to operate away from public roads

suspension: the system of springs supporting a dirt bike

terrain: an area of land and its natural characteristics and surface

throttle: a device that controls the flow of fuel to an engine

track: a special road or course set up for a race

Learn More

Britannica Kids: Motorcycle
https://kids.britannica.com/students/article
/motorcycle/275952

Conaghan, Bernard. *Motocross*. New York: Crabtree, 2023.

Dirt Bike Facts
https://xtrememotox.com/dirt-bike-facts/

Kaiser, Brianna. *Supermoto: Rev It Up!* Minneapolis: Lerner Publications, 2023.

Kiddle: Motorcycle Facts for Kids
https://kids.kiddle.co/Motorcycle

Mikoley, Kate. *Off-Road Racing*. New York: Gareth Stevens, 2020.

Index

enduro, 11
engine, 7, 12–13

motocross, 9, 11

supermoto, 9, 15
suspension, 16–17

tire, 17
trail racing, 9, 11
treads, 15

Photo Acknowledgments

Image credits: Hafizov/Getty Images, p. 4; grahamheywood/Getty Images, p. 5; PPstock/ Shutterstock, p. 6; Alex_Ishchenko/Getty Images, p. 7; Artur Didyk/Getty Images, p. 8; PeopleImages/Getty Images, pp. 9, 13; AnnaTamila/Shutterstock, p. 10; Cavan Images/Getty Images, p. 11; Fertnig/Getty Images, p. 12; Evan Raihan Rafi/Shutterstock, p. 14; Westend61/ Getty Images, p. 15; eggeegg/Shutterstock, p. 16; MoMo Productions/Getty Images, p. 17; Glowimages/Getty Images, p. 18; vm/Getty Images, p. 19; mladn61/Getty Images, p. 20.

Cover: Charlie Yacoub/Getty Images.